Helping Toby's Team

Sandra Fitzgerald
Illustrated by Peter Shaw

Toby's team needed lots of things for the baseball game.

"How will we carry everything?"
asked Toby.

"We can use my wagon!" I said.
"I'll pull it!"

We put everything in the wagon.

"It's heavy now," I said.

6

We went across the park.
I pulled the wagon onto the grass.
The wagon stopped!

9

"I can not move it," I said.

"You pull, and I'll push," said Toby.

We moved the wagon onto the path.

"I can pull it now," I said.

Toby's team was waiting.

"We have everything for the game!"
I said.

14

"Hooray!" said Toby's team.